SWEDISH COOKIES AND DESSERTS

© Bokförlaget Max Ström 2011
Text and recipes Malin Landqvist
© Photo Joel Wåreus
Translation Kim and Lukas Loughran
Design Victoria Bergmark
Factchecking, recipes Kristina Valentin
Proof-reading Kathryn Boyer
Repro Fälth & Hässler, Värnamo, Sweden
Printing Livonia Print, Latvia 2011
Second imprint
ISBN 978-91-7126-215-8
www.maxstrom.se

MALIN LANDQVIST

SWEDISH COOKIES

AND DESSERTS

PHOTO JOEL WÅREUS

TRANSLATION KIM AND LUKAS LOUGHRAN

BOKFÖRLAGET MAX STRÖM

We Swedes have reason to be proud of our cookies and cakes. Those hand-written scraps of paper with well-tried family recipes that have been passed down through generations up and down the country are an amazing cultural treasure. Many families have their 'very own' cinnamon buns or a real 'family cake'. Baking traditions recapture smells and tastes from our memories. It might be a cake with a scent that makes you dizzy with joy or perhaps a taste you recall but can't place. Suddenly, there you are, back in grandma's kitchen …

As I write, I hear the rain smattering on the roof here in Österlen (the Tuscany of Sweden!) in Skåne province and remember that my love for baking and cooking was nurtured here. My grandmother on my father's side baked wonderful cakes and was from Skåne, as were several of the ladies in the family, and most were terrific at baking. But my grandmother on my mother's side, from Gothenburg, baked the very best pepparkakor (ginger thins), crammed with ginger and lemon oil. The way they tasted is the way I feel ginger cookies should taste.

I have tried to write an inspiring, tempting book of simple recipes to give more people an appetite for our fantastic cookies and desserts. At first, I was almost smothered in ideas for the book's content, since there are so many goodies to choose from. How to select? Several wonderful treats did not make the cut. I wanted to show off both classic and modern delicacies. And obviously I also wanted to include some immigrant and some original recipes. The result is very personal.

May I wish you many enjoyable afternoon teas and coffee breaks!

Malin Landqvist

CONTENTS

THE 7 COOKIES

1 large batch:
1 litre / 15 oz / 4¼ cups plain flour
2 dl / 5.7 oz / 0.8 cup sugar
550 g / 20 oz room-temperature
butter
3 egg yolks (Save the egg whites
for glazing the cookies.)
½ dl / ¼ cup water if needed

Homemakers took pride in lavishing seven different kinds of cookies on friends and relatives. This recipe can make 150 cookies, at a stretch.

With a mixer: Put all the ingredients except for the water in the mixer bowl. Mix. Drizzle in water if the dough does not bind — you want a smooth, easy-to-handle dough. Let rest about 30 minutes in the fridge. By hand: Tip the flour onto a work surface. Make a hollow in the middle and fill with the sugar and butter. Pinch everything together until you get big crumbs. Add the egg yolks and knead into a dough. Add a little water if needed and follow the recipe above.

FINN STICKS

Egg white, pearl sugar, chopped sweet almonds

Roll out 1/7 of the dough, making a roll about as thick as a finger. Brush with lightly beaten egg white and sprinkle with pearl sugar and the chopped almonds. Cut out about 30 'sticks' and put them on a baking tray lined with oven paper. Bake in the middle of the oven at 175C/350F for about 10 minutes.

CINNAMON COOKIES

Egg white, cinnamon and sugar

Roll out 1/7 of the dough, to a roll about as thick as a thumb. Brush with lightly beaten egg white, sprinkle with cinnamon and sugar. Flatten slightly and slice diagonally into about 25 cookies. Bake at 175C/350F in the middle of the oven for about 10 minutes.

MINI-JITTERBUGS

Egg white and sugar

Roll out 1/7 of the dough between two sheets of greaseproof paper to make a rectangle of about 30 x 15 cm / 12 x 6 in. Peel away the upper paper. Whisk 1 egg white stiff. Add 1 dl / 3 ½ oz sugar and whisk until the mixture is hard and shiny. Spread half of it on the rectangle. Roll up the dough, long side to long side, with the help of the lower paper sheet, as for making swiss roll. Put the roll in the freezer for about 30 minutes. Cut into slices the thickness of a plastic CD case and put them on a baking tray lined with oven paper. Bake at 175C/350F in the middle of the oven for 10–12 minutes. Let cool on the tray.

TOSCA STICKS

Tosca topping:
50 g / 1.7 oz butter
½ dl / 1½ oz / 3⅓ Tbsp sugar
2 Tbsp honey
1 Tbsp plain flour
50 g / ½ cup flaked almonds

Roll out 1/7 of the dough to make a rectangle of about hardback book-size. Line with oven paper an ovenproof pan of about the same size. Melt the butter in a saucepan. Whisk in the sugar, honey and flour and stir for about a minute while it thickens. Add the almond flakes. Spread the topping on the dough and bake at 175C/350F in the middle of the oven for 15–20 minutes until the cake is golden brown. Watch carefully to see it doesn't burn. Let cool. Cut the cake in half lengthwise and then slice into about 20 sticks.

CHESS SQUARES

Cacao

Divide 1/7 of the dough into two equal bits. Work 1 Tbsp of cacao into one of them. Roll each into two snakes of about the thickness of a pinkie. Stretch out a dark and a light snake together. Put another light snake on top of the dark, a dark on top of the light. Squeeze them lightly together. Cut into slices about as thick as a CD case. On a baking tray lined with oven paper, bake at 175C/350F in the middle of the oven for about 10 minutes.

If you like, make 9 really thin snakes and shape a roll of three layers of alternating colours. Just make the slices thinner and reduce the baking time a little.

BRUSSELS BISCUITS

Egg white, sugar and red food colouring

Roll out 1/7 of the dough to make a roll about as thick as a garden hose. Brush with lightly beaten egg white. Mix the sugar and colouring and roll the roll in it. Slice about 1½ cm / ½ in thick. On a baking tray lined with oven paper, bake at 175C/350F in the middle of the oven for about 10 minutes.

CARDAMOM LEAVES

Egg white, cardamom seeds and pearl sugar

Roll out 1/7 of the dough thinly (about as thick as 2 stacked coins). Brush with lightly beaten egg white. Sprinkle with freshly ground cardamom seeds and pearl sugar. Stencil or cut out leaves or hearts and place on a baking tray lined with oven paper. Bake at 175C/350F in the middle of the oven for about 10 minutes until they begin to colour.

MALIN'S MINI LEMON LENTEN BUNS

100 mini or 25 large buns:
100 g / 3½ oz butter
3 dl / 10 fl. oz / 1⅓ cups milk
75 g fresh yeast / 7½ tsp dry yeast
½ tsp salt
1 dl / 2.8 oz / 0.4 cup sugar
1½ tsp crushed black cardamom
seeds (or ground cardamom)
1 egg
about 1 litre / 4¼ cups plain flour
1 tsp baker's ammonia / salt of
hartshorn
1 egg white for brushing
powdered sugar

Filling:
300 g / 10½ oz almond paste
2 Tbsp room-temperature butter
2 egg yolks
1 Tbsp cream
zest from 1 lemon
about 3 dl / 10 fl. oz / 1⅓ cups
whipping cream

Lots of yeast and baker's ammonia make these buns extra light and soft. You might think a batch of 100 is over-doing it, but they disappear in a flash, I promise! If you want to be traditional, make the buns big. They can be deep-frozen but not with the filling.

Melt the butter. Add the milk and warm to 'baby-bottle' temperature. Dissolve the yeast in the water and add salt, sugar, cardamom and the egg. Mix the baking powder into the flour then gradually add to the wet mix until you get a shiny, smooth dough. Allow to rise under a cloth for about 30 minutes. Prepare the filling in the meantime. Mix the almond paste, butter, egg yolks, 1 Tbsp cream and lemon zest until smooth. (If using a pastry / piping bag, fill it now.) Put to one side.

Heat the oven to 250C/480F. Knead the dough and roll into two lengths. Cut into bits then roll into roughly 100 small balls or 25 large ones. Put on a baking tray lined with oven paper. Brush the buns with whisked egg white. Bake small buns 3–5 minutes in the middle of the oven, 6–8 minutes for large ones. Let cool completely. Cut off the crown of each bun and scoop out a shallow hole. Whip the cream. Pipe or spoon in the filling and top with whipped cream. Replace the crown and powder with powdered sugar.

HOMEMADE ALMOND PASTE

For about 12 buns:
2 dl / 5 oz / 0.8 cup almonds
1–1½ dl / 2–3 oz / 0.4–0.6 cup
powdered sugar
1 egg white

Easy to make and a must for large-size Lenten buns. Blanch and peel the almonds if you like, but I prefer a slightly rougher paste.

Mix the almonds to fine crumbs in a food processor or in an old-fashioned nut mill. Add the powdered sugar and egg white and mix until you get a paste. Spoon into the hollows in the buns and top with whipped cream.

MALIN'S CRISPY WAFFLES

8–9 batches (about 30–35 waffles):
50 g / 1.7 oz butter + extra for frying
4 dl / 6 oz / 1.6 cups plain flour
2 tsp sugar
½ tsp salt
½ tsp baking powder
2 dl / 6.7 fl. oz / 0.8 cup whipping cream
1 dl / 3.3 fl. oz / 0.4 cup milk
2 dl / 0.8 cup mineral/soda water

Swedes mark Waffle Day on 25 March, coinciding with the Feast of the Annunciation or Lady Day, as winter segues into spring. Waffles have been popular in Sweden since the Middle Ages but were top culinary fashion at the turn of the previous century when weekend strollers would munch them at pavement kiosks. Waffles used to be made over open fire before the invention of the waffle iron. Swedes love round waffles that divide into heart shapes; other countries prefer square. Waffles are popular at markets and cafés and on the ski slopes.

Serve these straight from the iron. Or keep them on an oven rack before enjoying with lightly whisked cream and a good jam.

Melt the butter and let it cool. Mix the dry ingredients in a bowl. Add the melted butter, cream and milk and whisk until any lumps are gone. Pour in the mineral water and whisk gently until the batter is smooth. Heat the waffle iron and brush with butter. Butter the iron between batches.

⊙ Drop 3–4 ice cubes into the batter to keep it cold and make the waffles crispier. Using bubbly mineral water instead of tap water makes the waffles fluffier.

EASTER DESSERT-IN-A-JAR

8–10 portions:
Stewed rhubarb:
750 g / 1.6 lb rhubarb
1 little bit (ca 2 cm) fresh ginger
2 dl / 5.7 oz / 0.8 cup sugar

Yoghurt mousse:
4 dl / 13½ oz / 1.7 cups thick
yoghurt, Greek or Turkish (10%)
1 vanilla pod
1½ dl / 5 oz powdered sugar
2 dl / 7 oz whipping cream

Rhubarb tangle:
Peel off a few thin strands from the
rhubarb. Keep in ice water until
time to serve. Take them out and
tie into little tangled knots.

I love seeing dessert served in small glass jars or pots. This recipe layers thick, smooth vanilla yoghurt mousse with homemade stewed rhubarb. Nothing says 'spring' like this dish! Serve with a delicate cookie, like a Dream.

If your rhubarb is thick, peel; if it's thin, there's no need. Cut into 2 cm / 1 in pieces. Trim the ginger and cut into matchsticks. Put the rhubarb in a wide saucepan. Add the ginger and sprinkle with sugar. Let the rhubarb reduce over a low heat for 8–10 minutes. Allow to cool.

Put the yoghurt in a bowl. Divide the vanilla pod lengthwise and scrape out the seeds. Mix the seeds and the powdered sugar into the yoghurt. Whisk the cream and blend into the mix.

Carefully layer stewed rhubarb and yoghurt mousse in small glass jars or glasses. Garnish with mint, rhubarb tangle and grated or thinly sliced lemon zest.

⊙ Stewed rhubarb is fabulous on its own with cold milk, although a little crushed cardamom seed on top works too. In summer, add strawberry sections for a lovely breakfast dish.

GRANDMA NANCY'S EASTER CAKE

8–10 servings:
300 g / 10 oz almond paste
3 eggs
3 bitter almonds
zest of 1 orange

Garnish:
150 g / 5 oz dark chocolate
a dollop of butter
marzipan (see page 29)

I can't think of anything easier to bake, especially considering the wonderful, moist end-product. (I'm trusting Grandma would approve of the bitter almond that I've added for extra character.)

Heat the oven to 175C/350F. Grease a midsize spring-form pan and dust with breadcrumbs. Finely grate the almond paste and put it in a bowl. Break the eggs and add them. Grate the almonds and put them in too. Add the orange zest and stir until you get a smooth batter. With a fork, mash any lumps against the side of the bowl. Pour the batter into the springform pan and bake in the middle of the oven for 20–30 minutes until it sets and has some colour. Melt the chocolate and butter and spread on the cake. Garnish with marzipan figures or pretty leaves.

SOFT SPONGE CAKE

One big cake:
225 g / 8 oz room-temperature butter
2½ dl / 7 oz / 1 cup sugar
3 eggs
4 dl / 6 oz / 1.6 cup plain flour
2 tsp baking powder
1 tsp vanilla sugar (with real vanilla)

Flavouring:
zest and juice of 1 large lemon or orange
2 Tbsp ground cardamom
1 dl/0.4 cup finely grated dark chocolate
1 dl / 0.4 cup finely grated hazel-nuts

½ dl / 3⅓ Tbsp cacao

2 dl frozen berries

I couldn't write about Swedish cakes and cookies without including a soft sponge cake. For a lighter, feathery cake, follow the base recipe for the cream cake (see p. 63), but use the flavouring tips below.

Heat the oven to 175C/350F. Grease a cake pan and line with breadcrumbs. Beat the butter and sugar until porous. Mix in the eggs one at a time. Add the dry ingredients and flavouring. Pour in the pan, smoothing with a spatula. Bake in the lower part of the oven for 35–40 minutes. Test with a sharp knife to see if it's ready. Cool a little in the cake pan before tipping out.

TIGER CAKE

Mix ⅓ of the batter and 2 Tbsp cacao. Spread out half of the lighter batter in the cake pan. Spoon on the darker batter, covering finally with the rest of the lighter batter. Ripple with a fork for a marbled look.

BERRY CAKE

Spread the batter in a round pan. Strew 2 dl / 0.8 cup frozen berries on the batter, pressing them in slightly. Or make a pretty pattern with thin slices of apples or pears dipped in cinnamon.

⊙ Muffins: Distribute the batter between the twelve moulds in a muffin tray. Bake at 225C/435F in the middle of the oven for about 20 minutes.

CHOCOLATE-MINT OR CITRUS MACAROONS

About 16 macaroons:
200 g / 3½ oz / 0.8 cup almond paste
1 egg white

Buttercream:
125 g / 4½ oz room-temperature butter
1 egg yolk
1½ dl / 3 oz / 0.6 cup powdered sugar
1 tsp vanilla sugar

Mint chocolate:
50 g / 1.7 oz dark chocolate (70%), melted and slightly cooled
a few drops of peppermint oil

Lemon & white chocolate ganache:
50 g / 1.7 oz white chocolate, melted and slightly cooled
zest of 1 small lemon
optionally, 1 tsp cognac or Cointreau

Chocolate ganache:
150 g / 5⅓ oz / 1½ cups dark or white chocolate
20 g / 1½ Tbsp coconut butter

Go for one sort or make both. If both, double the recipe for bases. They can be freezer-stored. Decorate with candied leaves, mimosa sugar bell sprinkles or other sprinkles.

Heat the oven to 175C/350F. Finely grate the almond paste. Stir in the egg white with a fork until all lumps are gone. Make small circles about as wide as the top of a beer can on a baking tray lined with oven paper. Bake in the middle of the oven for about 8–10 minutes or until they start browning. Let cool.

Whisk up the buttercream. Add the flavouring to the mint chocolate or lemon & white chocolate. Keep in the fridge 20–30 minutes.

Mounting: Use a spatula to make peaks of buttercream on the smooth side of the cookie base. Chill in the fridge for a while so they are cold when you dip them in the chocolate. Melt the chocolate and coconut butter. Dip the macaroons. Garnish, if desired, then chill until time to serve.

⊙ For that professional look, spread the cream very evenly on the base — use a spatula dipped in hot water.

PRINCESS CAKE

Cake base:
cream cake recipe, see page 63

4 dl / 13½ fl. oz / 1.7 cups whipping
cream
1½ dl / 5 oz / 0.6 cup raspberry or
strawberry jam
1 rolled marzipan lid (approx. 200 g / 7 oz)
powdered sugar

Vanilla cream:
1 vanilla pod
2 dl / 7 fl. oz / 0.8 cup milk
1 dl / 3.3 fl. oz / 0.4 cup whipping
cream
2 egg yolks
¾ dl / ⅓ cup light corn syrup / golden
syrup
1 Tbsp cornstarch
3 gelatin sheets (2 g sheets)

Marzipan lid:
Here's an easy marzipan: Mix well
500g / 1lb almond paste, 3 dl / 1¼ cups
powdered sugar and ½ dl / 3½ Tbsp
light corn syrup/golden syrup. Carefully
drizzle in food colouring until the
marzipan develops the desired shade.
Roll out thin between two sheets of
stretch wrap.

The cake was named in honour of Swedish princesses Märtha, Margaretha and Astrid, all taught by domestic science teacher Jenny Åkerström in the early 20th century. This was apparently their favourite subject matter. Bake the sponge cake in a round, midsize pan. Let cool completely.

Halve a vanilla pod lengthwise and scrape out the seeds. Put both pod and seeds in a saucepan. Add the rest of the cream ingredients except the gelatin sheets. Beat, and simmer on a low heat while stirring, until the first bubble appears. Remove from the heat. Put the gelatin sheets in cold water and leave 5 minutes, then take them out and mix them into the vanilla cream until dissolved. Store in the fridge, stirring a couple of times, until completely cold. Leave in the fridge for about 2 hours to set. This can be done a day before. Take the previously prepared marzipan lid out of the fridge to bring to room temperature. Whip the cream, but not stiff. Blend ⅔ of the cream into the vanilla mix. Layer the cake bases and vanilla cream, adding raspberry jam not before the second layer. Smear vanilla cream around the cake, making a slight mound on the top. Attach the marzipan lid and store cool for 1 hour. Dust with powdered sugar and decorate.

⊙ Decoration: Swedes favour Easter bunnies in meringue and Easter eggs in marzipan. Edible flowers are cute, and decorative green herbs can be mixed with marzipan leaves.

MAMMA'S CARDAMOM CAKE

About 10 servings:
6 dl / 9 oz / 2½ cups plain flour
2½ tsp baking powder
2 dl / 0.8 cup sugar
1 Tbsp freshly ground cardamom seeds
100 g / 3½ oz room-temperature butter
2½ dl / 9 fl. oz / 1 cup milk

Sprinkles:
2 Tbsp pearl sugar
1 tsp cinnamon
½ tsp freshly ground cardamom seeds

When we were kids, mamma used to throw together this wonderful cake for evening tea. The cast-iron skillet was part of the ritual and seemed to make the cake tastier. My grandmother had the same recipe.

Heat the oven to 200C/390F. Grease a cast-iron skillet or regular, midsize round pan and dust with breadcrumbs. Mix the dry ingredients in a bowl. Add the butter in small bits and pinch into the flour. Add the milk and stir until you get a thick batter. Spread the batter in the pan and strew the sprinkles over. Bake in the lower oven for 30–35 minutes. Use a knife to check that the cake is dry in the middle.

Best when fresh!

MERINGUES

About 20 meringues:
3 egg whites
2 dl / 5.7 oz / 0.8 cup sugar
1 tsp vanilla sugar
a few drops of spirit vinegar

Incredibly simple. My kids love whipping leftover egg whites. It's important to bake meringues low in the oven so they don't brown.

Heat the oven to 100C/210F. Whip the egg whites very stiff with an electric mixer. Add the sugar, a couple of Tbsp at a time, while continuing to whip until the mix is shiny, stiff and forming peaks. Whisk in vanilla sugar and spirit vinegar. Transfer the batter to a pastry bag with a decorating tip. Pipe rings or little Easter bunnies on oven paper-lined baking trays. Bake low in the oven for 35–50 minutes until they feel light and detach easily from the oven paper.

Walnut meringues: At the end of whipping, mix in 1 dl / 0.4 cup of chopped walnuts. Spoon out the batter to form little peaks on the baking sheet.

Raspberry meringues: When the batter is ready, pour it into a pastry / piping bag. Using the handle of a wooden spoon, make a deep hole in the batter. Drizzle a couple of Tbsp of concentrated raspberry juice into the hole. Cover with the meringue batter. Squeeze out small peaks, some of which will be marbled by the juice.

⊙ Toss over sprinkles when the meringues are piped or spooned onto the baking tray. Or pipe out pointy-headed ghosts. After baking, use a thin brush and food colouring to paint the eyes.

COCONUT TOPS

About 20 tops:
50 g / 1.7 oz butter
2 eggs
1 dl / 2.8 oz / 0.4 cup sugar
approx. 5 dl / 2 cups desiccated
coconut
optional flavouring

Garnish:
melted chocolate
sprinkles / hundreds and thou-
sands

Flavouring:
For a Swedish yuletide look, add
2 pinches (0.5 g) saffron to the batter.
Lime zest adds zing.

Heat the oven to 175C/350 F. Melt the butter in a sauce-pan. In a bowl, carefully blend the eggs and sugar. Mix in the coconut, melted butter and any flavouring. Let the tastes mingle for about 10 minutes. Using your fingers, make little peaks, placing them on a baking tray lined with oven paper. Bake until they get a little tanned. Lift off the cakes before they cool and dip the tops into melted chocolate or dribble some on. Sprinkle with sprinkles if wanted. Cool.

⊙ Letting the batter rest allows the coconut to swell and makes it easier to shape the little peaks.

DREAMS

About 25 dreams:
50 g / 1.7 oz room-temperature
butter
1½ dl / 4⅓ oz / 0.6 cup sugar
2 dl / 5.7 oz / 0.8 cup plain flour
1 Tbsp vanilla sugar
½ tsp baker's ammonia / salt of
hartshorn (substitute: ½ tsp
baking powder + ½ tsp baking
soda)
½ dl / 3.3 Tbsp canola / rapeseed
oil / corn oil

Garnish:
pumpkin seeds or pistachios

These should not brown, so keep the oven temperature low. It's best to use an electric mixer for the batter — a food processor will not produce the same result.

Heat the oven to 150C/300F. Using an electric mixer, beat the butter and sugar until white and fluffy. Drizzle in the oil slowly while stirring continuously. Add the dry ingredients and mix the dough at low speed. Roll into about 25 balls and spread them out on baking trays lined with oven paper. If you like, press a few pumpkin seeds or pistachios into the dough balls. Bake in the middle of the oven for about 20 minutes until the dreams are dry and light. Let cool on the baking tray.

Baker's ammonia / salt of hartshorn (*hjorthornssalt*) is hard to get outside northern Europe. Use baking powder + baking soda. This helps the cookies rise a little. With baker's ammonia, you might experience a slight ammonia smell during baking, but it fades and will not affect the taste.

⊙ Flavour your dreams with the zest of 1 lime or of ½ lemon or orange. You can also use ½ g / 2 pinches saffron dissolved in a few drops of water. Or why not 1 tsp of cinnamon or ground ginger?

KLADDKAKA CHOCOLATE MUD CAKE

8–10 chunks:
75 g / 2.6 oz butter
2 dl / 5½ oz / 0.8 cup sugar
2 eggs
½ dl / 3½ Tbsp cacao powder
1 tsp vanilla sugar
1 pinch salt
2 dl / 3 oz / 0.8 cup plain flour

Kladdkaka means 'gooey cake' but this is an easy recipe: the ingredients are all simply mixed together. You should find everything you need in your kitchen supplies.

Heat the oven to 150C/300 F. Grease a midsize springform pan with butter, then line with bread-crumbs. Or line an ordinary baking tin with oven paper as in the picture. Melt the butter. Mix sugar, eggs, cacao, vanilla sugar and salt. Add butter, then flour. Pour the mixture into the springform pan and bake in the middle of the oven for 15–20 minutes. Check frequently by shaking the pan, waiting for a heavy wobble (indicating a moist centre) before removing from the oven. This will give the cake a perfect 'mudiness' when it has cooled slightly. Serve lukewarm with a dollop of cream.

⊙ Flavour with orange zest, finely chopped chilli pepper, mint essence, cinnamon, lime or nuts.

PECAN PIECES

30–35 cookies:
2 dl / ⅔ cup pecan nuts
+ extra for decoration
150 g / 5⅓ oz room-
temperature butter
2 dl / 10 oz / 0.8 cup dark brown
sugar
1 egg yolk
½ tsp sea salt
2¼ dl / 3.3 oz / 1 cup plain flour
½ tsp baking powder
1 tsp vanilla sugar

Heat the oven to 175C/350F. Chop the pecans. Whisk the butter and dark brown sugar until light and airy. Blend in the egg yolk and sea salt. Mix the dry ingredients and blend them into the batter. Shape roughly into balls and distribute over two baking trays. Halve the garnishing nuts and stick a piece on each cookie. Bake one tray at a time in the middle of the oven for about 9–11 minutes until the individual cookies have spread and the edges are colouring. Let the cookies cool on the tray. They keep well for a week in an airtight jar and can be deep-frozen.

⊙ There's an old saying: If there's sugar in the recipe, add a little salt; if there's salt, add a little sugar. I like that rule, but for this recipe I use a generous pinch of salt. It gives the cookies character and marries well with the pecans.

OSCAR II CAKE

About 12 servings:
Cake bases:
100 g / 1½ dl / ½ cup sweet
almonds
4 egg whites
1½ dl / 4⅓ oz / 0.6 cup sugar

Buttercream:
4 egg yolks
100 g / ½ cup sugar
2 dl / 6.7 fl. oz / 0.8 cup whipping
cream
150 g / 5⅓ oz cold butter

Nut brittle:
½ dl / 3½ Tbsp sweet almonds
¾ dl / 2 oz / 5 Tbsp sugar

Garnish:
50 g / ¼ cup roasted almond
flakes
edible flowers — violets, for
example

King Oscar (1829–1907) must have had a sweet tooth! This is a smooth, butter-rich cake with a chewy, tasty almond base and soft buttercream. To crown it, home-made nut brittle provides crunch.

Heat the oven to 175C/350F. Draw 3 cake-size circles on oven paper. Grease them. Grind the almonds finely in a food processor. Whisk the egg whites stiff. Add almonds and sugar; stir gently to a smooth batter. Spread the batter on the circles. Bake in the middle of the oven for about 15 minutes until golden brown.

In a stainless steel saucepan, heat the egg yolks, sugar and cream until the mixture thickens. Don't let it boil. Remove from the heat. Let cool for 10 minutes.

Roughly chop the almonds for the brittle. In a sauce-pan, melt the sugar until golden brown. Add the almonds and pour onto greaseproof paper to cool and set. In a mortar, crush most of the nut brittle into crumbs. Roughly chop the rest. Save for decoration.

Shave the cold butter and stir into the buttercream, a little at a time. Blend in the nut brittle crumbs.

On a dish, alternate almond base with buttercream. Butter the sides with it too. Put in the fridge (or, better yet, the freezer) for at least an hour. Remove shortly before serving. Garnish with chopped nuts, roasted almond flakes and flowers.

WILD STRAWBERRY TARTLETS

About 14 tartlets:
Dough:
4 dl / 6 oz / 1.6 cups plain flour
150 g / 5⅓ oz cold butter, diced
1 dl / 2.8 oz / 0.4 cup sugar
1 tsp vanilla sugar
2 egg yolks
1–2 Tbsp water

Vanilla custard:
1 vanilla pod
2½ dl / 9 fl. oz / 1 cup milk
2 egg yolks
½ dl / 1½ oz / 3½ Tbsp sugar
2 Tbsp cornstarch

Garnish:
fresh wild strawberries

Wild strawberries picked in the forest, fantastically sweet and packed with flavour, are the very best, but anywhere you can find them will do.

Put all the dough ingredients except the water into a mixer and mix until finely grained. With the mixer running, add the water through the opening until the dough balls. Press the dough thinly into tart moulds. Put in the freezer for about 30 minutes. Heat the oven to 225C/435F. Bake the tartlets in the middle of the oven for 10–14 minutes until golden brown. Let cool in their moulds.

Split the vanilla pod lengthwise. Put it in a saucepan and pour in the milk. Bring to a boil then remove from the heat. Remove the vanilla pod. In a bowl, beat the egg yolks, sugar and cornstarch fluffy. Blend the mix into the warm milk, and, whisking constantly, carefully heat until the sauce thickens. Do not allow to boil, otherwise the eggs will coagulate and the sauce will be gritty. Let cool completely.

Fill the moulds with vanilla custard and top with as many wild strawberries as you like.

Mould size?
Tartlet moulds come in many sizes, so the number of tartlets is only an estimate.

CRISPY RHUBARB PIE WITH VANILLA CUSTARD

8 servings:
200 g / 1⅓ cup rhubarb
1 package frozen, thawed filo pastry (270 g / ½ lb)
75 g / 2½ oz butter
½ dl / 1½ oz / 3⅓ Tbsp light brown sugar
1 Tbsp freshly ground cardamom seeds
powdered sugar

Vanilla custard:
1 vanilla pod
2½ dl / 9 fl. oz / 1 cup milk
2 egg yolks
⅔ dl / 2 oz / 4½ Tbsp sugar
2½ Tbsp cornstarch
50 g / 1.75 oz finely grated almond paste
1 Tbsp butter

Filo pastry is not especially Swedish, but rhubarb with vanilla custard is. Don't worry if the pastry rips — just patch it together. If you can't find filo pastry, use rolled-out puff pastry dough and prick the bottom with a fork. Fill with rhubarb and custard and bake according to the recipe instructions.

Begin with the custard. Split the vanilla pod lengthwise. Put it in a saucepan with the milk. Bring to a boil and remove from the heat. In a bowl, whisk the egg yolks, sugar and cornstarch until fluffy. Remove the vanilla pod from the milk. Temper the egg mixture with a little of the milk. Whisk the mixture into the milk in the saucepan. Warm, while gently stirring, until the sauce begins to thicken. Do not let boil or the sauce will curdle. Whisk in the almond paste and butter. Put aside.

Heat the oven to 200C/390F. Melt the butter. Carefully spread out the thawed filo. Put six sheets on top of each other in a midsize springform pan. Brush each sheet with butter and sprinkle with brown sugar and cardamom. Slice the rhubarb thin. Spread the custard on the pie bed and cover with the rhubarb. Sprinkle a little cardamom over. Cut away most of the filo overhang, but not all, for a pleasing effect. Brush the edges with the last of the butter. Bake the pie in the middle of the oven for 20–25 minutes until it has some colour. Take out and let cool. Carefully unlock the pan and transfer the pie to a dish. Dust generously with powdered sugar.

MALIN'S FLAG DAY CONFECTION

8 servings:
8 thin slices of sponge cake
1 dl / ½ cup elderberry cordial
(diluted)
approx. 12 fresh strawberries
glasses or cups holding about
1½ dl / ½ cup

Mousse:
2 dl / 6.7 fl. oz / 0.8 cup
whipping cream
200 g / 7 oz white chocolate
2 egg yolks, room temperature
optionally, a few drops of red food
colouring

Elderberry jelly:
1 gelatin sheet
½ vanilla pod
¾ dl / ⅓ cup concentrated
elderberry juice or cordial
½ dl / ¼ cup water

Sweden's national day, or Swedish Flag Day, is on 6 June. These easy confections sing of early summer days and work well as a buffet component. They can be prepared 1–2 days in advance. I like them coloured pink with red food colouring. Instead of sponge cake slices, you can try sponge fingers (the Savoy biscuits used in tiramisu). One biscuit per portion is enough.

Make small round shapes from the cake slices to fit the bottom of small glasses or cups. Drizzle the elderberry liquid over.

Whip the cream. Break the chocolate into pieces and melt gently in the microwave or in a bain marie. In a bowl, energetically beat the egg yolks while adding the melted chocolate. Blend a little of the chocolate mix into the cream, then the rest. Add the (optional) food colouring and stir to a smooth batter. Divide the mousse equally between the glasses. Cover with plastic wrap and leave in the fridge for 2–3 hours. All this can be done 1–2 days in advance.

Soak the gelatin sheet in cold water for about 5 minutes. Slice the strawberries thinly and top the mousse with them. Cut the vanilla pod in half lengthwise and scrape out the seeds. Put the vanilla seeds in a saucepan with the elderberry cordial and water. Melt at low heat while stirring. Remove the saucepan from the heat and let it cool slightly. Drizzle the jelly on the mousse. Put in the fridge for about 30 minutes to set.

ALMOND CORNETS

About 35 cornets:
100 g / 3½ oz / ½ cup almonds
100 g / 3½ oz room-temperature
butter
1 dl / 2.8 oz / 0.4 cup sugar
2 Tbsp honey
1 Tbsp milk
1 Tbsp whipping cream
2½ Tbsp plain flour

The finest cookies of all. Perfect with ice cream or a mousse, bringing a delicate brittleness and crunchy almond flavour.

Heat the oven to 175C/350F. Finely chop most of the almonds, leaving a few just roughly chopped. Put all the other ingredients in a saucepan. Simmer for 1–2 minutes while stirring (do not allow to boil). Blend in the almonds. Spoon out about 35 dollops spaced widely apart on baking trays lined with oven paper. Bake in the middle of the oven for 5–6 minutes until light brown, keeping careful watch!

How it's done: When the cornets come out of the oven, let them cool on the tray for about one minute until you can lift them off with a spatula or slice. Place them on the convex side of a muffin tray or on an upside-down glass. Shape them carefully — they set quickly. Shape the cornets into little baskets and fill them with ice cream and berries for a dainty and festive look.

Alternatively, let them set over a rolling pin or a bottle for a curved shape. Old-fashioned bakeries used to shape them into rolls after letting them set only seconds on the rolling pin or bottle. Allow to set, then pipe in the buttercream (see page 26). Store in the fridge. Dip the ends in melted dark chocolate. Allow to set again.

CHILLED RHUBARB-STRAWBERRY SOUP WITH CARDAMOM

About 4 servings:
200 g / 7 oz rhubarb (approx. 2 stalks)
3 dl / 10 fl. oz / 1⅓ cups concen-
trated rhubarb cordial
6 dl / 20 fl. oz / 2½ cups water
1 vanilla pod, split lengthwise
1 tsp freshly ground cardamom seeds
1½ tsp potato starch/cornstarch
½–1 dl / 1½–3 oz / 3½–7 Tbsp
sugar
approx. 10 strawberries

Serve with:
ice cubes
vanilla ice cream

A refreshing cold soup best served with vanilla ice cream and almond cookies. Perfect for hot summer days.

Rinse, then cut the rhubarb into matchsticks and put them in a bowl. Bring to a boil the rhubarb cordial, water, vanilla pod and cardamom. Add the potato starch after dissolving it in 2 Tbsp water. Pour the hot liquid over the rhubarb and sweeten with sugar to taste, stirring until it dissolves. Check sweetness carefully, since cordials have different sugar strengths and rhubarb acidity can vary. Taste check before and after the soup cools. Let the soup cool and store it in the fridge for a couple of hours to let it absorb the flavours and soften the rhubarb. Slice the strawberries and add them. For extra coolness, add ice cubes.

ALMOND COOKIES

About 30 cookies:
1 dl / 60 g / 2½ oz / ½ cup
almonds
1¾ dl / 3½ oz / ¾ cup powdered
sugar
50 g / 1.7 oz room-temperature butter
1 dl / 1½ oz / 0.4 cup plain flour
2 egg whites

Garnish:
About 15 almonds, halved

Heat the oven to 200C/390F. In a blender, mix the almonds and powdered sugar until you get crumbs. Transfer to a bowl and beat with the butter until light and fluffy. Blend in the flour and egg whites to make a thick batter. Spoon onto baking trays lined with oven paper. Put the halved almonds on top, one on each. Bake in the middle of the oven for 7–9 minutes until the cookies colour nicely, darkening at the edges. Let cool on the baking tray. Store in airtight jars. Lemon or orange zest adds a delightful taste note.

HOTCAKES

3–4 servings:
2½ dl / 4 oz / 1 heaped cup spelt
or plain flour
1 Tbsp vanilla sugar
1 Tbsp potato starch/cornstarch
½ tsp salt
2 eggs
5 dl / 17 fl. oz / 2 cups milk
1 Tbsp vegetable oil
butter for the skillet

Serve with:
muddled berries (warmed), vanilla
ice cream or lightly whipped cream

Put the dry ingredients in a bowl. Add the eggs and half the milk. Beat until smooth. Stir in the rest of the milk and oil. Leave the batter to swell for at least 15 minutes. This batter can be used for hotcakes or pancakes.

Fry the hotcakes in butter on both sides in a skillet or pancake griddle. Serve with warm berries and cream or ice cream.

⊙ Why use spelt flour? It's healthier and tastier. The hotcakes won't be rougher. Classic plain flour works well too.

MUDDLED BERRIES

Choose among summer berries or buy frozen ones and thaw. Stir with sugar until you get a chunky mash. Different berries need different amounts of sugar — the sweetest strawberries need only a spoonful or two while red currants, for example, need plenty!

SWEDISH SWISS ROLL

1 big roll (20–24 slices):

3 eggs

2 dl / 5.7 oz / 0.8 cup sugar

2 Tbsp boiling water

2 dl / 3 oz / 0.8 cup plain flour

1½ Tbsp potato starch / cornstarch

1½ tsp baking powder

½ tsp vanilla sugar

2 dl / 3 oz / 0.8 cup jam or muddled berries

A swiss roll is quick to make and, with my system, easy.

Heat the oven to 250C/480F. Whisk the eggs and sugar until fluffy. Pour in the boiling water. Mix the dry ingredients and sieve into the egg mixture, folding in carefully. Spread the batter evenly to the size of a newspaper page on a baking tray lined with oven paper. Bake in the middle of the oven for 5–7 minutes. Sprinkle sugar on greaseproof paper and turn the cake onto it. Carefully remove the oven paper. Spread your filling of choice on the cake and use the greaseproof paper to roll up the cake tightly. Wrap in kitchen foil and let the roll rest, with the join underneath, for at least an hour. Slice.

Dreamy roll: Add 1 Tbsp cacao to the batter. Mix 150g / 5 oz soft butter, 2 dl / 7 oz / 0.8 cup powdered sugar, 2 tsp vanilla sugar and 1 egg yolk to a smooth paste. Spread it on the cooled cake and roll up.

Christmas roll: Add to the batter 1 Tbsp of combined ginger, cinnamon, ground cloves and cardamom. Prepare as above, adding 2 pinches of saffron to the filling.

Forest berry roll: Add the zest of 1 lemon to the batter. Mix 3 dl / 1¼ cups of muddled forest berries with vanilla seeds. Spread on while still warm and roll up.

Apple-cinnamon roll: Add 1½ tsp cinnamon to the batter. Spread 3 dl / 1¼ cups applesauce on the cake when still warm and roll up.

◉ Pulling away the oven paper a problem? Brush it with ice-cold water. Spread jam and fresh berries on the cake while it is still warm, then roll it immediately. Wait until the cake has cooled before spreading on creamy fillings and fillings that melt. Cover the cake with a slightly damp kitchen towel while cooling; this helps the cake stay moist until the filling is spread and makes it easier to roll up.

Vary your roll. The easiest variation is to use a good jam you might have at home. A slice of swiss roll, a dollop of whipped cream, and some berries and you've got a simple pastry.

VANILLA PRETZELS

14 pretzels:
150 g / 5⅓ oz room-temperature
butter
2 Tbsp sugar
½ dl / 3⅓ Tbsp whipping cream
4 dl / 6 oz / 1.6 cups plain flour
+ extra for working the dough
1 Tbsp vanilla sugar

Garnish:
milk
pearl sugar

Beat the butter and sugar until light and porous. Add the rest of the ingredients and work until you get a smooth dough. Store in the fridge for 30 minutes. Heat the oven to 175C/350F. Divide the dough into 14 bits and roll them into thin snakes, about 25 cm / 10 in long. Twist into pretzels and transfer to a baking tray lined with oven paper. Brush the pretzels with a little milk and sprinkle generously with pearl sugar. Bake in the middle of the oven for about 11–14 minutes until they just start colouring. Let them cool slightly on the baking tray, then transfer to an oven rack to complete cooling.

CHOCOLATE & SALTED PEANUT BISCUITS

35–40 biscuits:
1 dl / ½ cup salted peanuts
2½ dl / 4 oz / 1 heaped cup plain
flour
½ dl / 1½ oz / 3½ Tbsp sugar
150 g / 5⅓ oz cold butter
50 g dark chocolate (70% cacao)
1 egg yolk
1–2 Tbsp water as needed

In a food processor, mix the nuts finely. Add flour, sugar and butter chopped into pieces. Mix until you get a grainy dough. Chop the chocolate fine. Add the chocolate and the egg yolk to the dough. Mix, drizzling in water until you get an even, smooth dough. On a work surface, form the dough into a roll about the thickness of a banana. Chill for at least 30 minutes.

Heat the oven to 175C/350F. Slice the dough thin (about as thick as a coaster). Put the slices on a baking tray lined with oven paper and bake in the middle of the oven for about 10 minutes, keeping a close eye on them, until they colour nicely. Let cool on the tray.

CREAM CAKE

10–12 pieces:
Cake base:
50 g / 1.7 oz butter
2 dl / 3 oz / 0.8 cup plain flour
½ dl / 1 oz / 3⅓ Tbsp potato
starch / cornstarch
1 tsp baking powder
1 tsp vanilla sugar
4 eggs
2 dl / 5.7 oz / 0.8 cup sugar
½ dl / 3½ Tbsp water

Filling:
1 batch of vanilla custard
(see Wild strawberry tartlets, page 47)
½ punnet / 1 pint / ¼ lb berries
or 2 dl / 7 oz / 0.8 cup chopped
pineapple or 1½ dl / 5 oz /0.6
cup jam (strawberry, raspberry or
blueberry)
optional: sugar for the berries

Garnish:
1 punnet / 1 pint / ½ lb seasonal
fruit and berries, e.g. strawberries,
raspberries or nectarines
3 dl / 10 fl. oz / 1⅓ cups
whipping cream
strawberry or wild strawberry leaves

Light, fruity and deliciously creamy. Perfect with cordial with clinking ice cubes, coffee and cookies.

Heat the oven to 175C/350F. Grease and line with breadcrumbs a round, midsize pan. Melt the butter. Mix the dry ingredients. Whisk the eggs and sugar fluffy in a bowl for about 5 minutes. Pour the water into the melted butter and bring to a boil. Add to the egg mix. Fold in the dry ingredients and stir to a smooth batter. Pour into the pan. Bake in the middle of the oven for about 40 minutes. Let cool.

Prepare the vanilla custard and let it cool. Muddle the berries for the filling with a little sugar. Whip the cream. Cut large fruit into small pieces for decoration.

Mounting: Divide the cake into three bases. Spread the fruit filling on the bottom base. Place the next base on top, and spread vanilla custard on it. Add the final base and spread the whipped cream on top and around the sides. Decorate with fruit, leaves and / or flowers. Fill a pastry bag with the whipped cream and attach a star tip. Pipe cream 'roses' around the cake.

Cake bases can be baked and frozen for later use. Assembling a cake like this is called 'mounting'. Bake the cake a day in advance but wait until the day it will be eaten before spreading on the cream and berries. Vary, using muddled berries in summer and jam or pineapple in winter.

CARDAMOM KNOTS

About 40 knots:
150 g / 5⅓ oz butter
5 dl / 17 fl. oz / 2 cups milk
100 g fresh yeast / 3⅓ Tbsp dry yeast
1 tsp salt
1 dl / 2.8 oz / 0.4 cup sugar
1 Tbsp crushed cardamom seeds
14–15 dl / 6–6⅓ cups plain flour

Filling:
100 g / 3½ oz room-temperature butter
1 dl / 2.8 oz / 0.4 cup sugar
1 Tbsp ground cardamom

Garnish:
1 beaten egg
pearl sugar

1 Tbsp ground cinnamon

Melt the butter. Add the milk and warm to 'baby-bottle' temperature. In a bowl, dissolve the yeast in the water. Add the salt, sugar, ground cardamom and almost all the flour. Work the dough until shiny and smooth. Allow to rise under a cloth for about 40 minutes. Heat oven to 225C/435F. Mix the filling. Knead the dough on a lightly floured work surface. Halve, and roll the bits into rectangles, about the size of a spread magazine. Spread the filling on the rectangles. Fold the long edges to meet. Use a pizza cutter or a knife to make 2 cm / 1 in-wide ribbons. Stretching them slightly, twist the ribbons then tie into loose knots. Put them on baking trays lined with oven paper. Allow to rise under a cloth for about 30 minutes. Brush the buns with beaten egg and sprinkle with pearl sugar. Bake in the middle of the oven 8–10 minutes. Cool on an oven rack under a cloth.

CINNAMON BUNS

Cinnamon buns, the most popular way. Roll out the dough as above. Exchange cinnamon for the cardamom in the filling and spread on the dough sheet. Roll up the dough and cut into slices of about 3cm / 1 in. Put the slices in paper cupcake shapes. Allow to rise and then follow the recipe.

Other delicious fillings: Roughly grated almond paste, butter and small pieces of apple; butter, powdered sugar and both cinnamon and cardamom.

BLACK CURRANT PARFAIT

About 6 portions:
1 vanilla pod
4 egg yolks
1½ dl / 4⅓ oz / 0.6 cup sugar
1 egg white
3 dl / 10 fl. oz / 1⅓ cups
whipping cream
1½ dl / 5 oz / 0.6 cup black
currant jam
zest of 1 lemon

Garnish:
fresh white and / or black currants,
mint or lemon balm

Split the vanilla pod lengthwise and scrape out the seeds. Put the seeds in a bowl with the egg yolks and sugar, and set aside. Whisk the cream. Whisk the egg yolks frothy. Stir them into the cream with the jam and lemon zest. Carefully fold in the egg whites. Pour the batter into a rectangular pan (about 1½ litres / 50 fl. oz) or a cake pan. Keep in the freezer to set for at least 5 hours or overnight.

Put the parfait in the fridge for 30 minutes before serving. Tip onto a dish and garnish with fresh berries.

Flavour variation: Replace the black currant jam with seasonal jams or preserves. Decorate with that fruit.

GOOSEBERRY COMPOTE

4 portions:
600 g / 21 oz / 6 cups red or
green gooseberries
1 vanilla pod
1½ dl / 5 fl. oz / 0.6 cup water
about 1 dl / 2.8 oz / 0.4 cup
sugar
½ tsp ground cardamom seeds
12 tsp potato starch / cornstarch

Serve with:
50/50 whipping milk and cream

Half 'n' half — whipping cream and milk — really fits with berry compotes.

Dress the gooseberries and cut them in half. Split the vanilla pod lengthwise. In a saucepan, put the gooseberries, vanilla pod, the water and cardamom seeds. Bring to a boil and simmer for 3–6 minutes until the gooseberries soften slightly. Dissolve the potato starch / cornstarch in a little cold water and put it into the compote while stirring. Let cool. Serve with cream and milk.

Sweeten carefully. Gooseberries, like most berries, vary in sweetness. If you need more sugar, wait until near the end of preparation.

QUICK SQUARE CAKE WITH BERRIES

About 20 servings:
zest of 2 limes
juice of 1 lime
250 g / 8.8 oz butter
6 eggs
7 dl / 20 oz / 3 cups sugar
7 dl / 10 oz / 3 cups plain flour
4 dl / 6 oz / 1½ cups fresh or
frozen berries

Garnish:
powdered sugar
fresh berries and leaves

Mix the batter quickly and pour it into the pan — it cannot be easier! Because there is no baking powder, this is a compact, chewy cake. It is best when still a little sticky inside, so don't bake too long. Serve with vanilla ice cream or lightly whipped cream.

Heat the oven to 200C/390F. Spread oven paper on the bottom of an oven pan. Grate the zest and squeeze the juice from one of the limes. Melt the butter in a saucepan. In the meantime, beat the egg and sugar in a bowl for about a minute. Add the butter, flour, lime zest and juice and stir until you have a smooth batter. Pour the batter into the oven pan and sprinkle with berries. Bake in the middle of the oven for about 20 minutes. Use a knife to test when it's ready — it should be just a little sticky in the middle. If needed, tent with oven foil towards the end. Let cool and powder with powdered sugar. Fresh berries and leaves make a nice decoration.

⊙ Roll the lime hard against a work surface to make it easier to extract the juice. Cut it in half and squeeze.

CHOCOLATE TRUFFLE CAKE WITH CURRANTS

About a dozen servings:
Base: 400 g / 14 oz almond paste
100 g / 3½ oz dark chocolate
1 Tbsp cacao
1 egg
2 egg whites

Milk chocolate truffle:
300 g / 10½ oz good quality milk chocolate
200 g / 7 oz good quality dark chocolate
3 dl / 10 fl. oz / 1⅓ cups whipping cream
½ dl / 3⅓ Tbsp black currant or raspberry liqueur

Garnish:
berries, edible flowers, e.g. nasturtiums

Heat the oven to 175C/350F. Put oven paper on the bottom of a springform pan. Lock the pan. Mix the almond paste and chocolate in a food processor. Put the mix in a bowl and stir in the cacao, egg and egg whites. Spread the batter evenly in the pan. Bake in the lower part of the oven for 15 minutes. Let cool completely. Loosen the cake from the pan and remove the oven paper. Return the cake to the pan, smooth side up.

Break the chocolate for the truffle into bits. Bring the cream to a boil, then remove from the heat and add the chocolate. Stir until you get a smooth batter. Warm over low heat if the chocolate does not melt. Stir in the liqueur. Pour the batter over the cake base in the pan and put it in the fridge to set for at least 5 hours or overnight.

With a sharp knife, cut along the edges and loosen the pan. Decorate with berries and flowers.

⊙ Break the chocolate into bits while it's still in the packaging.

BAKED CINNAMON APPLES

Six servings:
6 midsize apples
1 dl / 2½ oz / ½ cup hazelnuts,
almonds or shelled and unsalted
pistachios
100 g / 3½ oz almond paste
2 Tbsp honey
3 Tbsp room-temperature butter

Garnish:
optionally, 6 cinnamon sticks

Serve with:
vanilla ice cream, cream or vanilla
custard

Autumn apples, soft and tart, are best for this.

Heat the oven to 200C/390F. De-core the apples so there's a hole right through. Put them in a greased oven pan. Finely chop the nuts or run them in a blender. Add the other ingredients and blend or stir until you get a stiff purée. Stuff the apples with the purée. Push a cinnamon stick into each for decoration and flavour. Bake in the middle of the oven for 20–30 minutes, depending on the kind of apple and size. When the skin starts to crinkle, they're done. Let cool slightly. Serve with vanilla ice cream, lightly whipped cream or custard.

Cooking time may vary. An apple with porous flesh will cook quicker than a firm one. Tent with oven foil if the apples start getting too dark.

POACHED SPICED PLUMS WITH BLACK-BERRIES

About 6 portions:
1 kg / 2.2 lb plums
about 15 blackberries

Syrup:
1 vanilla pod
8 dl / 27 fl. oz / 3⅓ cups water
2 star anise
1 cinnamon stick
5–6 dl / 14–17 oz / 2–2½ cups sugar

Serve with:
whipping cream or ice cream

Poaching plums is fun — with a pretty and very tasty result. The poached fruit can be kept in the fridge for about a week. Adjust the amount of sugar to the sweetness of the plums.

Split the vanilla pod lengthwise. Boil the water with the vanilla pod, star anise, cinnamon stick and sugar in a large saucepan. Let it reduce for about 10 minutes.

In the meantime, halve the plums and discard the stones. Put the plums in the syrup and simmer 1–2 minutes if the fruit is very firm; if the fruit is ripe they don't need go in the simmering syrup at all. Put the plums in strong glass jars. (Easiest using a perforated ladle.) Layer with the blackberries. Pour over the hot syrup. Leave to cool for at least a couple of hours.

Serve with a little whipping cream or ice cream.

PEAR PIE AND BLACKBERRIES

6–8 pieces:
175 g / 6 oz butter
3 dl / 4.4 oz / 1⅓ cups plain
flour
1 dl / 2.8 oz / 0.4 cup sugar
½ tsp baking powder
1 tsp vanilla sugar
1 generous pinch of salt

Filling:
3–4 medium-firm pears
1 Tbsp cardamom seeds
2 Tbsp sugar

Decoration:
1 dl / 5 oz / 0.4 cup smooth
apricot jam
fresh blackberries

Quick to make — just mix the dough and press it into the pie dish for an expert result. Crush cardamom seeds in a mortar for extra taste. Marmalade adds to the presentation and provides a tang, but can be skipped. Serve with homemade custard (see opposite page).

Heat the oven to 225C/435F. Melt the butter in a saucepan. Mix in the rest of the ingredients. Press everything into a midsize springform pan. Slice the pears thin, lengthwise, without removing the core. Overlap slices prettily in the pie shell. Crush the cardamom seeds and toss sugar and seeds over the pear. Bake in the middle of the oven 20–25 minutes until the sides are golden brown. Melt the marmalade in a saucepan with 1 Tbsp water. Brush on the pie. Let cool and decorate with fresh blackberries.

⊙ Use this dough for all kinds of pies. Just go with seasonal fruit. If it's soft fruit, like blueberries or currants, increase the baking powder to 1 tsp for a lighter dough. And toss the fruit in 1 tsp potato starch / cornstarch before putting into the shell.

VANILLA CUSTARD

Makes 4 dl / 14 fl. oz:
1 vanilla pod
2 dl / 6.7 fl. oz / 0.8 cup heavy
or double cream
1 dl / 3.3 fl. oz / 0.4 cup milk
5 egg yolks
¾ dl / 2 oz / ⅓ cup sugar + a
little extra

◉ *Strew a little sugar on the*
surface when the custard is ready,
to stop it forming a skin. Alumi-
nium can affect the colour of the
custard, so use a stainless steel pot.

Incredibly better than store-bought custard powder!
Great with apple cake or other pies and desserts.

Split the vanilla pod and scrape out the seeds. Pour
the cream and milk into a stainless steel saucepan,
adding the vanilla pod and seeds. Bring to the boil
then remove from the heat. Meanwhile, whisk the
egg yolks and sugar for several minutes until white
and porous. Remove the pod from the milk mixture.
Add some to the whisked eggs so they don't congeal
as you whisk the mixture into the saucepan. Heat,
stirring constantly, until it thickens slightly. Don't let
it boil. Strain the custard through a fine-meshed
strainer and allow to cool. Store cold until serving.

BEETROOT CAKE WITH LEMON FROSTING

10–12 pieces:
2 large beetroots
1¾ dl rapeseed / canola oil
1 dl / 3½ oz dark muscovado sugar
1½ dl / 4½ oz / 0.6 cup light brown sugar
2 eggs
2½ dl / 4 oz / 1 cup plain flour
½ Tbsp cinnamon
1½ tsp baking powder
¼ tsp salt

Frosting:
1 vanilla pod
200 g cream cheese (Philadelphia type)
100 g / 3½ oz room-temperature butter
4 dl powdered sugar
finely grated peel of 1 lemon

A moist cake, gorged with finely grated beetroot. The topping is a classic frosting. Garnish with petals from edible flowers such as marigolds, nasturtiums and violets.

Heat the oven to 175C/350F. Peel and finely grate the beetroot, making 4 dl / 1¾ cups. This is easiest done in a food processor. Squeeze gently to get rid of excess juice. In a bowl, whisk the oil and sugars (brown and muscovado) for a minute or so. Whisk in the eggs one at a time. Mix the dry ingredients then blend them into the batter with the beetroot. Pour into a midsized rectangular bread pan that has been lined with oven paper or greased and dusted with breadcrumbs. Bake in the middle of the oven 25–35 minutes. Check with a knife for the moment when the inside sets and it's beautifully moist. Remove and leave to cool completely.

Halve the vanilla pod lengthwise and scrape out the seeds. Put the seeds in a bowl with the rest of the frosting ingredients and whisk until fluffy. Spread on the cake. Garnishing suggestion: flower petals.

⊙ Try other root vegetables. Swap the beetroot for an equal volume of carrot. Use light muscovado sugar.

BLACKBERRY GROTTOES

18 grottoes:

Dough:

125 g / 4½ oz butter

½ dl / 1½ oz / 3½ Tbsp
powdered sugar

2 dl / 3 oz / 0.8 cup plain flour

½ dl / 3 ½ Tbsp custard powder

½ tsp baking powder

brioche moulds

Filling:

blackberry jam

Frosting:

1 dl / 2 oz / 0.4 cup powdered
sugar

½ Tbsp water

Jam grottoes are among Sweden's favourite cakes. Raspberry is the most common flavour, but this is an autumn variation using blackberries. Pipe frosting over them or dust with powdered sugar.

Heat the oven to 200C/390F. Put all the dough ingredients into a food processor and blend. (If the dough doesn't stick together, add 1–2 tsp water.) Roll out a snake and slice into 18 pieces. Roll them into balls and put in brioche moulds. Put them on a baking tray and press a deep dimple in each. Put a teaspoonful of jam in each dimple. Bake in the middle of the oven for 7–9 minutes until they start to colour. Let cool. Mix the frosting and transfer to a piping / pastry bag. Pipe frosting on the cakes. Store in jars or deep-freeze.

BIRTHDAY BROWNIES

About 20 pieces:
1 vanilla pod
200 g / 7 oz good quality dark chocolate
200 g / 7 oz butter
4 eggs
1 dl / 0 .4 cup light muscovado sugar
2 dl / 5.7 oz / 0.8 cup sugar
2 dl / 3 oz / 0.8 cup plain flour
1 tsp baking powder
2 pinches salt

Garnish:
50 g / 1.75 oz white chocolate

Chocolate-choked, moist brownies. With a thin crust and creamy heart, they melt in your mouth. I make lots, just to see that mountain of brownies on the dish! Best baked a day in advance.

Heat the oven to 200C/390F. Line a rectangular pan with oven paper. Halve the vanilla pod lengthwise and scrape out the seeds. Break the chocolate into pieces. Melt the butter in a saucepan. Put in the vanilla seeds and chocolate and let melt. Whisk the eggs, muscovado and white sugar in a large bowl until fluffy. Mix the dry ingredients. Blend the dry ingredients with the chocolate-butter mix and the egg-and-sugar mix and stir gently until smooth. Spread the batter evenly in the pan. Bake in the middle of the oven for about 15 minutes. The cake should have a soft centre and not be baked through. Let cool completely before serving.

Melt the white chocolate. Let it cool a little so it's easier to pipe. If you don't have a pastry / piping bag use a thick plastic bag. Cut a tiny hole in the corner and pipe the chocolate over the cake.

⊙ Strew over 1 dl salted peanuts before baking. The interplay between salted, crunchy nuts and smooth, sweet cake is fantastic. For a Swedish Christmas feel, add generous pinches of mixed cinnamon, ginger, ground cloves and cardamom.

MALIN'S 'VACUUM CLEANERS'

About 25 vacuum cleaners:
300 g / 10 oz marzipan, ready-made or see page 29
food colouring

Filling:
50 g / 1.7 oz room-temperature butter
about 7 dl / 3 cups sponge cake crumbs
1 Tbsp cacao
1–2 Tbsp Swedish punsch (or arak essence)

Chocolate:
100 g / 3½ oz dark chocolate
20 g / 1½ Tbsp coconut butter

A beloved cake with many names, but it looked just like a 1950s model Electrolux vacuum cleaner, so the name stuck. This is my 'mini' version.

Good to make if you have a little semi-stale, leftover sponge cake. Or mix cake crumbs with cookie crumbs (the proportions depend a little on the kind of crumbs).

Stir together butter and cake crumbs. Add cacao and punsch or arak and work until you get a manageable chocolately mass, adding more crumbs if necessary. Roll out into four snakes about 2 cm / 1 in in diameter. Store in the freezer for the time being. Knead the food colouring into the marzipan. With a rolling pin, shape two thin rectangles of the same length as the snakes, between two sheets of greaseproof paper. Peel away the top sheet. Roll a snake in the marzipan, cutting when it is covered. Repeat. Cut into thumb-long cylinders. Melt the chocolate and coconut butter. Dip the ends in chocolate and let set. Store cool.

⊙ If you don't have cake crumbs handy, stir together the following ingredients: 8 digestive biscuits and 1½ dl / ½ cup rolled oats crushed into crumbs in a food processor. Stir in 75 g / 2½ oz soft butter, 100 g / 3½ oz grated marzipan, 1 dl / ⅓ cup powdered sugar, 1 Tbsp cacao and 1–2 Tbsp punsch or arak. Shape into rolls and follow the recipe above.

DANISH PASTRIES

About 30 pastries:
1 batch vanilla custard,
see page 47
optionally, a little raspberry jam

Dough:
25 g / 1 oz cold butter
50 g fresh yeast / 5 tsp dry yeast
2½ dl / 9 fl. oz / 1 cup milk
1 egg
zest of 1 small lemon
½ dl / 1½ oz / 3½ Tbsp light brown sugar
½ tsp salt
8–9 dl / 12–13⅓ oz / 3⅓–3¾ cups plain flour

Filling:
300 g / 10½ oz room-temperature butter

Frosting:
2 dl / 3.8 oz / 0.8 cup powdered sugar
1½ Tbsp water

Make sure all the ingredients for the dough, including the flour, are cold.

Make the vanilla cream and let it cool. Dice the dough butter. Put all ingredients except the flour in a bowl, ideally a food mixer with a dough hook. Add 2 dl / 3 oz / 0.8 cup of flour and mix carefully to a smooth dough. Store cold for about 15 minutes.

Roll the dough to a rectangle, about 35 x 45 cm / 14 x 18 in, on a floured work surface. Cut the filling butter into 10 slices. Spread these over one half of the rectangle, keeping the edges free. Fold the edges over the butter, then fold over the other half of the rectangle. Pinch the edges together. Roll the dough again on a floured work surface with a firm, steady hand, making a rectangle about 1 cm / ½ in thick. Roll from the middle out from both directions. Fold a third of the rectangle towards the middle. Repeat from the other side so you have three layers. Roll out again. (If the dough splits, don't worry.) Turn the rectangle 90 degrees. Fold to get three layers again. Repeat. Store the layered dough in the fridge for 15 minutes.

Roll out the dough to make a rectangle about 1 cm / ½ in thick 50 x 30 cm. Cut out about 30 strips and twist them. Make ovals or eights and put them on a baking tray lined with oven paper. Spoon or spread the vanilla custard on them. Optionally, dab a little raspberry jam on each. This is as far as you go if you want to save the pastries in the freezer to bake-off later. Cover the pastries loosely with plastic wrap. Leave to rise for 40 minutes. Heat the oven to 225C/435F. Bake the pastries in the middle of the oven for 8–10 minutes until they colour nicely. Remove from the oven and let cool briefly. Mix the frosting and dribble over the pastries. Serve freshly baked.

Bake-off: Because Danish pastries are best freshly baked, I have made the recipe bake-off-ready. After they have risen, freeze the pastries on a flat surface. When coffee break comes around, grab as many pastries as you need from the freezer and bake immediately at 225C/435F for 10–15 minutes.

KRONANS KAKA THE CROWN'S CAKE WITH LEMON CREAM

About 10 servings:
250 g / 1⅓ cups of a floury
variety of potato — boiled, peeled
and cold
150 g / 0.8 cup sweet almonds
6 bitter almonds
300 g / 10 oz room-temperature
butter
2½ dl / 7 oz / 1 cup sugar
4 eggs
1 dl / 1½ oz / 0.4 cup plain flour
zest of ½ lemon

Lemon cream:
2 egg yolks
2 Tbsp powdered sugar
2 dl / 6.7 fl. oz / 0.8 cup
whipping cream
zest of ½ lemon
a few drops of fresh lemon juice

Cold boiled potatoes in the batter provide beautiful moisture. In hard times and for soldiers, cooks had to substitute potato for flour. But use a floury variety of potato; the waxy kind will produce a gluey consistency.

Heat the oven to 175C/350F. Grease and dust with flour a midsize springform pan. If you don't have a potato ricer handy, use a grater for the potatoes. Grind the almonds in a nut grinder or mix them fine in a food processor. Whisk the butter and sugar until white and porous. Blend in the eggs one at a time, then blend in the potato and almonds. Lastly, mix in the flour and lemon zest. Spread the batter in the spring-form pan and bake in the lower oven for 40–50 minutes. Let cool in the pan.

Lemon cream: Whisk the egg yolks and powdered sugar until porous. Add the cream and whisk for several minutes until the sauce is creamy and thick. Add the lemon zest and juice. Serve with the cake.

CHOCOLATE TOFFEE COOKIES

About 40 cookies:
100 g / 3½ oz room-temperature
butter
1 dl / 2.8 oz / 0.4 cup sugar
½ dl / 3 Tbsp light or corn syrup
2 Tbsp cacao
2¼ dl / 3.3 oz / 1 cup plain flour
+ a little extra to work with
½ tsp baking soda
1 tsp vanilla sugar
1 pinch of salt

This popular recipe comes from the Swedish cook-book doyenne Anna Bergenström. When I had my restaurant in Stockholm these were the guests' favourite cookies. I've adapted Anna's recipe by adding extra syrup for chewiness and also a pinch of salt.

Heat the oven to 175C/350F. Whisk the butter, sugar and syrup fluffy with an electric mixer. Mix the dry ingredients in a bowl, then add the butter-sugar-syrup. Mix to a loose dough. Divide in half and make two rolls about 50 cm / 20 in long. Flatten the rolls, first by hand then with a fork. Bake in the middle of the oven for 15–20 minutes until the dough begins to split. Remove and let cool slightly. Cut into diagonals and let cool completely.

VANILLA ICE CREAM DE LUXE

5–6 servings:
1½ sheets of leaf gelatin or equiva-
lent amount of agar-agar
3 dl / 10 fl. oz / 1⅓ cups milk
2 dl / 6.7 oz / 0.8 cup thick cream
1 vanilla pod
½ dl / 3½ Tbsp honey
6 egg yolks
½ dl / 3½ Tbsp sugar

⊙ *If you want to chill the ice cream*
quickly put the bowl in another
bowl semi-filled with icy water and
perhaps some ice cubes. Freshen the
cold water occasionally and the ice
cream will cool quickly.

A creamy, vanilla-rich ice cream. Served with deep dark chocolate sauce and crispy Cat Tongues, it's yummy! Agar-agar powder works like gelatin and is completely plant-based. Can be found in health food stores. (Gelatin is made from animal by-products, agar-agar from seaweed.)

Soak the gelatin sheets in cold water for about 5 minutes. Pour the milk and cream into a large, thick-bottomed pan. Halve the vanilla pod lengthwise and scrape out the seeds. Put the vanilla seeds and pod into the pan with the honey. Bring to a boil, then remove from the heat. Whisk the egg yolks and sugar until white and porous. Whisking continuously, pour the egg batter into the warm vanilla-milk. Pour the batter into the pan. Heat gently, stirring constantly, until it thickens. (Do not boil!) Remove and immediately transfer to a cold bowl. Squeeze all water from the gelatin sheets and add to the ice cream mix. Allow to cool. Remove the vanilla pod.

Run the mix in an ice cream machine for about 40 minutes or put the bowl in the fridge, stirring now and then.

DEEP-DARK CHOCOLATE SAUCE

About 2 dl / 1 cup sauce:
1 dl / 3½ oz good quality cacao
1 dl / ½ cup water
1 dl / 2.8 oz / 0.4 cup sugar
a pinch of gourmet salt

Remember '1+1+1' and you'll remember the recipe. Piece of cake! Whisk the cacao, water and sugar in a saucepan. Bring to a boil, whisking until smooth. Crush a little sea salt in your fingers and toss it in.

CAT TONGUES

About 25 tongues:
50 g / 1.7 oz room-temperature
butter
1 dl / 2.8 oz / 0.4 cup sugar
2 egg whites
1 dl / 1½ oz / 0.4 cup plain flour
almond flakes

These are special: delicate, simple, and great with ice cream.

Heat the oven to 200C/390F. In a bowl, whisk the butter and sugar until white and porous. In another bowl, and using a fork, beat the egg whites. Add to the first bowl. Then add the flour and stir to a smooth batter. Pour into a pastry / piping bag. Pipe out lengths of 7 cm / 3 in on a baking tray lined with oven paper. Make them wide at the ends, thin in the middle. Toss over some almond flakes. Bake the cakes in the middle of the oven for 6–8 minutes or until the edges start to brown.

STINA'S CONES

About 14 cones:
100 g / 3½ oz room-temperature
butter
1½ dl / 4⅓ oz / 0.6 cup sugar
2 egg whites
2½ dl / 4 oz / 1 heaped cup
plain flour
½ tsp vanilla sugar
optional: a pinch of cinnamon

Filling:
lightly whipped cream
lingonberry or cloudberry jam

I get a warm feeling inside every time I remember Stina, the cook at my daycare when I was little, making cones for us kids. She made them with lingonberry cream, but you can vary the filling. It's real handicraft work and your fingers get hot!

Heat the oven to 200C/390F. Beat the butter and sugar until porous. Using a fork, lightly whisk the egg whites. Add flour, vanilla sugar and egg whites and blend to a smooth batter. Make thin discs about 12 cm / 5 in in diameter, on baking trays lined with oven paper. Dust with a little cinnamon if you like. Bake in the middle of the oven for about 5 minutes, when they should start to colour. Take out the tray and shape them, one by one, into cones. Put the cones in a mug or similar while they harden. Then fill with cream and jam.

⊙ If the discs start to stiffen too quickly, put the baking tray back in the oven for a quick burst. Be careful, because your fingers can get very hot very quickly.

CLOUDBERRY CONES

Filling:
1 dl / 3½ oz / ½ cup cloudberry
jam
200 g / 7 oz / 0.8 cup Philadel-
phia cheese
1 dl / 3.3 fl. oz / 0.4 cup
whipping cream
zest of ½ orange

Beat the filling ingredients until porous, using an electric mixer. Pipe or spoon the filling into the cones immediately before serving.

MAZARINS

About 12 mazarins:
dough: 2½ dl / 4 oz / 1 heaped
cup plain flour
½ tsp baking powder
1 tsp vanilla sugar
100 g / 3½ oz cold butter
1 egg yolk
1 tsp water if needed
oval cupcake moulds (metal or
paper)

Filling:
2 bitter almonds
2 dl / 5 oz / 0.8 cup sweet
almonds
50 g / 1.7 oz room-temperature
butter
1 dl / 2.8 oz / 0.4 cup sugar
2 eggs
flavouring of choice

Frosting:
1½ dl / 3 oz / 0.6 cup powdered
sugar
½ Tbsp water
or
table sugar

Put the dry ingredients for the dough in a food processor. Dice the butter and add it, together with the egg yolk. Mix until you get a ball (drizzling in water if needed). Press the dough into the moulds and store in the fridge for about 30 minutes.

While waiting, prepare the filling. Finely grate the bitter almonds. In a food processor, mix the sweet almonds to crumbs, or grind them in a nut mill. In a bowl, stir together the bitter almonds, butter and sugar. Lastly, stir in the egg and optional flavouring.

Heat the oven to 175C/345F. Put the moulds on a baking tray and fill. Bake in the middle of the oven for 15–17 minutes until they have a little colour. Mix the frosting and spread on the cakes. Let cool, or turn in sugar first. Store in jars or deep-freeze.

Flavouring: Citrus zest is perfect. Use the juice instead of water in the frosting.

⊙ To get that authentic Swedish *konditori* look, tip the mazarins upside down onto oven paper as soon as they come out of the oven. Let them rest for about 15 minutes, to give them a nicely flat top. Spread on the frosting.

TOSCA CAKE

1 large cake:
125 g / 4½ oz butter
½ dl / 3⅓ Tbsp milk
2 dl / 5.7 oz / 0.8 cup light
brown sugar
3 eggs
3 dl / 4.4 oz / 1⅓ cups sieved
spelt or plain flour
1 tsp baking powder

Tosca topping:
150 g / 5½ oz / 1⅓ cups mixed
nuts (e.g. hazelnuts, pistachios,
cashews and almonds)
100 g / 3½ oz butter
2 Tbsp milk
½ dl / 1½ oz / 3½ Tbsp light
brown sugar
2 Tbsp honey
1 Tbsp plain flour

Heat the oven to 175C/350F. Grease a midsize springform pan and line with breadcrumbs. Melt the butter for the cake in a saucepan. Pour in the milk. Beat the brown sugar and eggs until fluffy. Mix the flour and baking powder and blend into the egg mixture with the milk and butter. Stir until you get a smooth batter, then pour into the cake pan. Bake low in the oven for 25 minutes. While waiting, prepare the topping. Chop the nuts and almonds. Mix the other ingredients in a saucepan and melt over a low heat. Simmer for a couple of minutes, stirring all the while, until the mix thickens a little. Do not boil. Blend in the nuts. Remove the cake from the oven and carefully spread the topping on it. Bake in the middle of the oven for another 10–15 minutes until it has some colour. Test with a knife to see if it comes out clean.

MALIN'S ROSEHIP SOUP

About 1.2 litres / 2.5 pints:
5 dl / 2 cups dried rosehips
½ vanilla pod
1 cinnamon stick
12 dl / 5 cups cold water
2 dl / just less than 1 cup orange
juice (without fruit fibre)
1–2 dl / 3–5.7 oz / 0.4–0.8 cup
light brown sugar
1–2 Tbsp honey

⊙ *Double-straining. The standard*
recipe does not call for double-strain-
ing, but the flavour is deepened by
straining and then mixing some of
the pulp into the soup, then straining
again. Too much pulp makes the
soup bitter.

About 80 macaroons:
100 g / 3½ oz / 0.4 cup finely
grated almond paste
½ dl / 3½ Tbsp sugar
1 egg white
flaked almonds

Powdered rosehip soup is available, but it's far too sweet. If you can find dried rosehip (try health food stores), making the soup isn't hard.

Put the rosehips in a large saucepan. Split the vanilla pod, scrape out the seeds. Add seeds, pod and cinnamon stick. Pour in the water and soak for 3–4 hours.

Pour in the juice and bring to a boil. Simmer covered for about 5 minutes. Remove from the heat and stir in the smaller amounts of sugar and honey. Strain the soup through a fine-mesh sieve. Put just under 1 dl / 3½ oz of the rosehips into the soup, holding back the vanilla and cinnamon stick. Mix the soup in a food processor. Strain the soup again. Taste-check for desired sweetness. Dilute with water if needed.

ALMOND MACAROONS

To make the macaroons slightly chewy, I use more egg white than the traditional recipe. They're even chewier when you dip them in hot rosehip or blueberry soup.

Heat the oven to 200C/390F. In a bowl, mix the almond paste and sugar. Whip the egg white lightly with a fork and blend into the almond paste mix. Spoon onto a baking tray lined with oven paper or use a pastry bag to pipe small blobs. Stick an almond flake in each. Bake in the middle of the oven for 8–10 minutes until golden. Let cool on the tray.

SWEDISH CHEESECAKE

6–8 portions:
1 dl / 2½ oz / 0.4 cup almonds
+ a few for decoration
1 vanilla pod
500 g / 17½ oz / 2 cups ricotta
or white cheese
2 dl / 6.7 fl. oz / 0.8 cup
whipping cream
2 eggs
1 dl / 1½ oz / 0.4 cup plain flour
1⅓ dl / 3.7 oz / ½ cup sugar
zest and juice of 1½ lemons

Serving:
powdered sugar
lemon zest
whipped cream
fresh or frozen berries, heated

Classic Swedish cheesecake uses rennet. I've used a modern replacement, ricotta, for its creaminess, but you can go with white cheese. Watch the cake carefully near the end so it doesn't set too much — you want some 'bounce' inside when you take it out of the oven.

Heat the oven to 175C/350F. Grease small moulds or a large pie pan and line with breadcrumbs. Chop the almonds roughly, putting some aside. Split the vanilla pod lengthwise and scrape out the seeds.

In a bowl, stir the vanilla seeds thoroughly with chopped almonds and the rest of the ingredients. Pour the batter into the pan or moulds and sprinkle with the remaining almonds. Bake in the middle of the oven for 20–35 minutes or until it has just set. Test by shaking the pan or a mould gently. Allow to cool but serve slightly warm, dusted with powdered sugar and lemon zest. Lightly whipped cream and heated berries suit beautifully.

APPLE CRUMBLE WITH LINGONBERRIES

4 portions:
400 g / just under 1 lb / 2 cups
apples
butter for greasing the pan
1 dl / ½ cup lingonberries /
cranberries
½ dl / 3⅓ Tbsp light brown
sugar
½ tsp ground ginger

Crumble dough:
150 g / 5⅓ oz cold butter
3 dl / 4.4 oz / 1⅓ cups plain
flour
½ dl / 0.8 oz / 3½ Tbsp
roughly chopped hazelnuts
½ dl / 0.8 oz / 3½ Tbsp
pumpkin seeds
½ dl / 0.8 oz / 3½ Tbsp
sunflower seeds
2–3 Tbsp light brown sugar

A variation of a classic apple crumble, with nuts and seeds added for extra crunch. Adjust the amount of sugar to the sweetness of your apples. I use a medium-sweet apple variety. Apples with thin peel don't have to be peeled. Serve with vanilla ice cream or lightly whipped cream.

Heat the oven to 225C/435F. Core the apples and chop into small pieces. Grease an oven dish (or 4 small bowls) generously with butter. Put in the apples and toss over lingonberries, sugar and ginger.

Dice the butter and pinch it into the flour to get a coarse dough. Add the rest of the dough ingredients and mix. Spoon onto the apples and bake in the middle of the oven for about 20 minutes until the apples soften and the crumble is golden.

Fruit alternatives: Replace apples with the same volume of rhubarb, currants, gooseberries or other fruit. Just remember that sour fruit needs more sugar than you might think, and very soft fruit should be rolled in about 1 Tbsp potato flour so it doesn't go runny.

⊙ Let ½ litre / 1 pint of good quality ice cream thaw a little. Whisk 3 dl / 10 fl. oz / 1⅓ cups whipping cream and stir with the ice cream until fluffy.

VANILLA HEARTS

12–14 hearts:
1 batch cold vanilla custard,
see page 47
powdered sugar
metal moulds for the hearts

Dough:
5 dl / 7½ oz / 2 cups plain flour
1½ dl / 4⅓ oz / 0.6 cup
powdered sugar
½ dl / 1 oz / 3⅓ Tbsp potato
starch / cornstarch
1 tsp vanilla sugar
1 large pinch salt
200 g / 7 oz butter
1 egg yolk

Put the dry ingredients for the dough in a food processor. Dice the butter and add it. Mix until you get a grainy dough. Add the egg yolk and mix until smooth. Divide in two and press half the dough into the moulds. Scrape the edges clean. Put the moulds and the remaining half of the dough in the fridge for about 30 minutes.

Heat the oven to 200C/390F. Take the moulds and dough out of the fridge and spread the vanilla custard in the moulds. Roll out the lump of dough on a floured work surface and, using a mould as a template, cut out heart-shaped bits to be the lids. Cover the open moulds, pressing down the edges and even them out. Bake in the middle of the oven for about 15 minutes until they just start to colour. Let cool, then slide the hearts carefully from their moulds. Powder lavishly with powdered sugar. Serve cold but freshly baked.

GINGER-MARMALADE CAKE

10–12 servings:

150 g / 5⅓ oz butter

3 eggs

2 dl / 6 oz / 0.8 cup sugar

*1½ dl / 4½ oz / 0.6 cup dark
brown sugar*

4 dl / 6 oz / 1.6 cups plain flour

2½ tsp baking powder

2 tsp ground ginger

2 tsp cinnamon

2 tsp ground cardamom

2 tsp ground cloves

*2 dl / 6.7 fl. oz / 0.8 cup sour
cream, double cream or buttermilk*

*¾ dl / 3.8 oz / ⅓ cup marma-
lade*

A pleasingly moist, soft ginger cake.

Heat the oven to 175C/350F. Grease and dust with breadcrumbs a midsize sponge cake dish. Melt the rest of the butter and let cool slightly. In a bowl, whisk the eggs and the sugar and dark brown sugar until porous, using an electric mixer if you have one handy. Mix the dry ingredients. Blend them into the egg mixture together with the sour cream / double cream / buttermilk and marmalade until smooth. Tip into the cake dish. Bake in the lower oven for 50–65 minutes until it feels dry. Tent with foil for the final minutes if needed.

Flavours: My recipe uses orange marmalade for the citrus tang, adding a gentle tartness. Lingonberries (or cranberries) work well and are traditional too.

Resist opening the oven door too early. If the cake sinks, it won't rise again.

⊙ Don't over-bake. Test with a small, sharp knife when close to finish — the knife should come out moist but clean. Keep a close eye on the oven; the cake can bake dry in a flash.

LEMON BUTTONS WITH LIQUORICE

About 120 little buttons:
100 g / 3½ oz room-
temperature butter
zest of 1 large lemon
½ tsp vanilla sugar
½ dl / 1½ oz / 3½ Tbsp sugar
2½ dl / 4 oz / 1 heaped cup
plain flour

Liquorice sugar:
½ dl / 1½ oz / 3½ Tbsp sugar
1½ Tbsp liquorice paste

Lemon and liquorice, what a combo! Liquorice paste (alternatively, liquorice root) is available at specialty spice and essence shops. You can also skip the liquorice and make just lemon buttons. In which case, mix the sugar with extra lemon zest.

Using an electric beater, whisk the butter, lemon zest, vanilla sugar and ordinary sugar until light and porous. Add the flour and beat at low speed until you get a grainy mix. Tip it onto a work surface and knead it until you get a proper dough. Mix the sugar thoroughly with the liquorice paste (or lemon zest) by rubbing it between the palms of your hands. Roll out to make four thin snakes about 1½ cm / ½ in thick. Brush lightly with cold water and roll them in the liquorice (or lemon) sugar. Place on a tray and store cool for about 2 hours. Heat the oven to 175C/350F. Cut the snakes into slices about as thick as a coaster and spread out on baking trays lined with oven paper. Bake in the middle of the oven for 7–10 minutes until lightly coloured. Let the buttons cool on the baking tray.

SAFFRON-LEMON TWIRLS

Makes 35–40 twirls:
Basic dough:
5 dl / 2 cups plain flour
1 dl / 2¼ oz / 0.4 cup potato
flour / cornstarch
2 ½ dl / 1 cup powdered sugar
1 tsp vanilla sugar
225 g / 8 oz cold butter, diced

Flavouring 1:
zest from 1 lemon
1 Tbsp lemon juice

Flavouring 2:
0.5 g / 2 pinches powdered saffron
1 Tbsp hot water

Not classics, but should be. In Sweden, saffron and Christmas belong together so I made a saffron cookie. They are not hard to make, but give yourself time.

Put the ingredients for the basic dough in a mixer bowl. Mix to fine crumbs. Take out half and reserve. To the rest, add flavouring #1 and mix until you get a grainy dough. On the baking board, knead until smooth and even. Put the dough you had saved back in the mixer. Dissolve the saffron in hot water and add it. Mix until you get another grainy dough. On the baking board, quickly knead until smooth.

Roll out the dough on oven paper, making 2 rectangles about the size of a standard laptop. Carefully place one on top of the other, dough on dough. Peel away the top sheet of paper and, starting from the edge of the long side, gently make a compact roll of the dough. Use the paper underneath to help. Refrigerate for about 30 minutes.

Heat the oven to 175C/350F. Slice the dough to roughly the thickness of a plastic CD case and place on a baking tray lined with oven paper. Bake in the middle of the oven for 10–12 minutes or until slightly golden.

⊙ When mixing the basic dough, use a kitchen scales to get equal halves.

FARMER'S SHORTBREAD

About 60 cookies:
150 g / 5⅓ oz room-
temperature butter
100 g / ¾ cup almonds
2 Tbsp light or corn syrup
1½ dl / 4⅓ oz / 0.6 cup sugar
4 dl / 6 oz / 1.6 cups plain flour
¾ tsp baking soda
1 Tbsp water if needed

Melt a third of the butter in a saucepan till it starts browning and has a nutty scent. Remove from the heat and let cool. Chop the almonds. Place all ingredients, including the melted butter, in a bowl. Using an electric mixer, blend until smooth. If slightly dry, add 1 Tbsp water. Shape into two thick snakes (approx. 4 cm / 1½ in thick) and store in the refrigerator for about an hour. Cut the snakes into finger-thick slices with a sharp knife and place on baking trays lined with oven paper. Bake in the middle of the oven for 8–10 minutes at 200C/390F. Let cool on the tray.

⊙ Browned butter gives a wonderful, slightly nutty flavour. Use a food processor to prepare the dough quickly and easily. Chop the almonds first.

LEMON-CINNAMON DIAMONDS

40–50 cookies:
200 g / 7 oz room-temperature butter
1½ dl / 4⅓ oz / 0.6 cup sugar
½ dl / 3 Tbsp light or corn syrup
5 dl / 7½ oz / 2 cups plain flour
2 Tbsp vanilla sugar
2 tsp baking powder
1 tsp cinnamon
1 tsp ground ginger
zest of 1 lemon or orange

Lemon, ginger and cinnamon are all good for a sore throat, so crunch into some of these with a hot cup of tea when you get your next cold.

Heat the oven to 175C/350F. Whisk butter, sugar and syrup in a bowl until porous. Mix all dry ingredients and add, with the zest, to the butter mix. Knead to a smooth, heavy dough. Roll into four lengths of approx. 50 cm / 20 in. Place on baking trays lined with oven paper and flatten them slightly. Bake in the middle of the oven for 13–15 minutes. Let cool slightly before cutting into verticals.

KÄRLEKSMUMS LOVE-YUMMIES

About 24 squares:
225 g / 8 oz butter
5 eggs
4 dl / 12 oz / 1.7 cups light
brown sugar
¾ dl / 2½ fl. oz / ⅓ cup canola
oil or sunflower oil
¾ dl / 2½ fl. oz / ⅓ cup milk
4½ dl / 6½ oz / 2 cups plain flour
1½ dl / 2½ oz / ½ cup cacao
2½ tsp baking powder

Frosting:
100 g / 3½ oz butter
1 dl / 3⅓ fl. oz / ½ cup strong
coffee
½ dl / 1 oz / ¼ cup cacao
1½ tsp vanilla sugar
6 dl / 11½ oz / 2½ cups
powdered sugar

Garnish:
about 2 dl / 2⅓ oz / 0.8 cup
shredded coconut

These show up often at parents' day at schools, and kids love to bake them. Swedes also call them mocha squares. (Love-yummies is cuter!)

Heat the oven to 175C/350F. Melt the butter in a saucepan. Beat the eggs and sugar light and porous in a bowl. Add the melted butter, oil and milk. Mix the dry ingredients and sieve them into the batter. Stir carefully until smooth. Pour into an oven pan lined with oven paper. Bake in the middle of the oven for 20–25 minutes. Let cool in the pan.

Melt the butter for the frosting and pour in the coffee. Whisk together with the other frosting ingredients and spread on the cake. Strew over shredded coconut.

⊙ Children's party?
Colour the coconut green so it becomes a lawn and decorate with little marzipan animals.

HAZEL TOPS

About 35 cookies:
50 g / 1.7 oz butter
200 g / 1 cup hazelnuts
1 dl / 2.8 oz / 0.4 cup sugar
1 egg
hazelnuts for decoration

Simple and classic. Can be baked several ways. This way is uncomplicated and produces an astonishingly good result!

Heat the oven to 175C/350F. Melt the butter and let it cool slightly. In a food processor, mix the nuts to fine crumbs. Add the melted butter, sugar and egg. At low speed, blend into a thick mass. Using two teaspoons, spoon the mix onto baking sheets lined with oven paper. Top each cookie with a whole or half hazelnut. Bake the cookies in the middle of the oven 12–15 minutes. Let cool on the tray. Store airtight in a jar.

⊙ Ideal for gluten avoiders. To be old-fashioned, grind the nuts in a mixer. Another version uses whipped egg whites, folded into the dough.

VANILLA HORNS

About 40 cookies:
5 dl / 7½ oz / 2 cups plain flour
200 g / 7 oz room-temperature butter
2 Tbsp vanilla sugar (ideally with real vanilla)
1–2 tsp cold water if needed

Garnish:
sugar

Delicate, light cookies. The dough is a little dry, so they can be tricky to shape. You need a soft and nimble touch!

Put the flour in a bowl with the butter and vanilla sugar. Beat with an electric mixer. Transfer the resulting dough to a work surface and shape into two rolls (adding water if needed). Cut each into about 20 pieces. Carefully roll into thick slugs, a little thinner at the ends. Gently bend them into horns. Transfer to a baking tray and store cold for about 15 minutes.

Heat the oven to 175C/350F. Place the horns on baking trays lined with oven paper. Bake in the middle of the oven for 12–14 minutes. They should only just brown! Turn them in sugar while still hot. Let them cool completely on a rack.

Store the cookies in an airtight jar. They can also be deep-frozen.

⊙ If the sugar won't stick to the cookies, brush first with a thin coat of egg white, which works as glue.

SAFFRON BUNS

About 35 buns:
1 g / 4 pinches powdered saffron
1 lump of sugar or 1 Tbsp pearl
sugar
150 g / 5⅓ oz butter
4 dl / 13½ fl. oz / 1.7 cups milk
50 g fresh yeast or 5 tsp dry yeast
250 g / 1 cup buttermilk cheese /
creamed cottage cheese / curd
cheese
1½ dl / 5 fl. oz / 0.6 cup light
corn syrup / golden syrup
1 egg
½ tsp salt
14–16 dl / 6–6¾ cups plain flour
optionally, chopped raisins

Egg wash and decoration:
raisins
1 beaten egg

Swedes have been baking with saffron for a thousand years and it is strongly associated with Advent and Christmas. Each province used to have its own saffron cake. The spice comes from a special crocus species and is the world's costliest, so in the old days, cakes were brushed with syrup with saffron in it. This dough delivers moist, golden-yellow buns.

Using a mortar and pestle, pound the saffron and sugar well. Melt the butter in a saucepan. Add milk and heat to 'baby-bottle' warm. Crumble the yeast in a bowl (ideally, a mixer bowl) and dissolve in the milk. Add the creamed cottage cheese, syrup, egg and salt. Add most of the flour and, optionally, the chopped raisins. Mix the dough for about 5 minutes. Cover with a cloth and allow to rise for 40 minutes. Form into shapes and poke the raisins deep inside. Set the oven to the desired temperature (see guide). Let the buns rise under a cloth for another 20 minutes. Brush with the beaten egg, then bake. Let the buns cool on the oven tray under the cloth.

Small buns — in the middle of the oven for 6–8 minutes at 250C/480F. Midsize buns — in the middle of the oven for 10–15 minutes at 225C/435F. Big buns — in the middle of the oven for 15–20 minutes at 200C / 390F.

⊙ Don't use too much flour; the dough should be loose so the buns turn out nicely moist. Be careful not to bake too long; keep checking. Let them cool on the baking tray under a cloth. Freeze as soon as they're cool.

MALIN'S GINGER THINS

140–160 thins:
1½ dl / 5 fl. oz / 0.6 cup light or corn syrup
2 Tbsp cinnamon
1 Tbsp ground cloves
a few drops of bitter orange extract / oil
2 tsp ground cardamom
1 tsp ground ginger
250 g / 8.8 oz room-temperature butter
2 dl / 5½ oz / 0.8 cup sugar
½ tsp lemon oil (optional)
6½–7½ dl / 2.7–3 cups sieved spelt or plain flour
1½ tsp baking soda

Swedes love using cookie cutters to make figures and shapes. The year's first batch usually goes in the oven on the first Sunday of Advent. Round ginger thins are fine, but here, we're making figures. Take the dough out of the fridge about an hour before making the figures or shapes.

Day 1: Heat the syrup and spices in a saucepan until just about to boil. Remove from the heat to cool slightly. Whisk butter and sugar until white and fluffy. Add the spiced syrup and, optionally, the lemon oil. Mix the baking soda into the flour. Add the butter mix and knead to a smooth dough. Halve the dough, cover the bits with stretch wrap and keep in the fridge for at least 24 hours.

Day 2: Let the dough soften at room temperature for at least 1 hour before using. Heat the oven to 200C/390F. Roll out the dough on a floured surface and cut out shapes, freehand or with cookie cutters. Swedes love cut-outs of pine trees, stars, crescents, gingerbread men and women, and — pigs! Put the cookies on a baking tray lined with oven paper and bake in the middle of the oven for 5–7 minutes.

⊙ Lemon oil is a concentrate of dried citrus peel. A drop or two gives the cookies great resonance and delicate taste. It's available where essential oils are sold. Try sieved spelt flour. It acts like plain flour but has a fuller taste and adds nutrition.

FROSTING

2 dl / 3.8 oz / ¾ cup powdered
sugar
1 Tbsp egg white
1 ml / 1/3 tsp spirit of vinegar
or lemon juice
optionally, food colouring

Loose frosting is hard to pipe properly, so measure the amount of egg white accurately. My recipe might seem short on egg white but keep whisking and it'll get smooth and a little heavy. Transfer to a pastry / piping bag or thick plastic bag. If using a plastic bag, cut a tiny hole and test-pipe onto a surface. Enlarge the hole if you need to; it's easier to start small and enlarge the hole than to start over with a new bag. Spirit vinegar or lemon juice gives the frosting a fine shine.

Whisk the ingredients together. An electric mixer will give you a lump-free, smooth sugar mixture. If you want colour, add a few drops of red, green or yellow food colouring.

⊙ Good cookery shops stock the disposable pastry / piping bags that bakeries use. Fill, then cut a little hole in the tip. You can also use a thick plastic bag. But don't double-bag two thin ones; you might get two holes instead of one.

LINGONBERRY PEARS WITH CHOCOLATE CARAMEL SAUCE

6 servings:
5 dl / 17 fl. oz / 2 cups water
3 dl / 4½ oz / 1⅓ cups lingon-
berries / cranberries, frozen or
fresh
6 firm pears
juice of 1 lemon
1 vanilla pod
3 slices fresh ginger
4 dl / 11 ½ oz / 1.7 cups sugar

Chocolate caramel sauce:
1½ dl / 5 fl. oz / 0.6 cup
whipping cream
1 dl / 2.8 oz / 0.4 cup sugar
1 Tbsp butter
1 dl / 3⅓ fl. oz / 0.4 cup light
syrup
½ dl / 3⅓ Tbsp cacao
½ tsp vanilla sugar
50 g / 1.7 oz dark chocolate
(70%)
1 large pinch gourmet salt

The pears can be prepared a couple of days in advance. They're good served cold with a little of the syrup and hot chocolate sauce.

Boil the lingonberries in the water for about 10 minutes. Peel the pears and put them in a bowl with water, adding the lemon juice to stop the fruit going brown. Split the vanilla pod and scrape out the seeds. Put pod and seeds in the lingonberry water with the ginger and sugar and bring back to the boil. Put in the pears and simmer until they just begin to soften in the syrup. This takes 20–30 minutes. Take out the pears, using a perforated ladle, and transfer to a large glass jar. Reduce the syrup for about 5 minutes. Pour over the pears. Let cool.

Put all the sauce ingredients except the chocolate and salt in a saucepan. Whisk while heating to dissolve the cacao. Let the sauce reduce over medium heat for about 10 minutes. Remove from the heat and crumble in the chocolate. Stir until melted. Crush the salt in your fingers and add, stirring.

When are the pears done? Test with a sharp knife, looking for a slight resistance in the fruit. They will soften further in the syrup.

⊙ This sauce is astonishing with vanilla ice cream and fresh berries. You can also reduce by cooking an extra 5 minutes to create a fabulous layer-cake filling.

ALMOND TARTS WITH CLOUDBERRY JAM

About 45 tarts:
100 g / 3½ oz / 0.4 pint sweet
almonds
6 bitter almonds
200 g / 7 oz room-temperature
butter
1½ dl / 3 oz / 0.6 cup superfine
sugar (or blend ordinary sugar for
about 60 sec.)
6 dl / 9 oz / 2½ cups plain flour
1 egg
butter for the tart moulds

Serve with:
lightly whipped cream
cloudberry jam

In Sweden, these are a special Christmas treat. Swedes have special moulds with a fluted edge, but you can use regular small tart moulds. The cloudberry jam component is typically Swedish. Other berries — fresh or frozen, then warmed — are delicious too.

Blanch and peel the sweet and bitter almonds. Grind them in a food mill or as finely as possible in a food processor. In a bowl, mix butter and sugar until porous. Add all ingredients and mix into a smooth, elastic dough. Shape into a thick log. Cover with stretch wrap and put in the fridge for about 30 minutes. Heat the oven to 200C/390F. Grease the tart moulds with butter. Cut the dough into about 45 slices. Press the slices into the moulds and put on an oven tray. Bake in the middle of the oven for 8–10 minutes until the cookies brown nicely. Let cool a while then carefully extract from the moulds. Let cool completely on an oven rack. Serve with lightly whipped cream and warmed berries.

⊙ Cookie dough and cookies can be freezer-stored. Unless you have a lot of tart moulds, bake the cookies in batches. Divide the dough into portions and freeze what you're not using. Let the dough thaw before pressing it into the moulds.

CHRISTMAS CHEESECAKE AND LINGONBERRIES

About 10 servings:
Base:
150 g / 5⅓ oz butter
300 g / 10 oz ginger thins

Filling:
1 vanilla pod
400 g / 1½ cups cream cheese /
white cheese
2 dl / 0.8 cup crème fraîche
2 eggs
½ tsp (total) ginger, cardamom,
ground cloves and cinnamon
2 Tbsp cornstarch
¾ dl/2 oz / 5 Tbsp / ⅓ cup
sugar

Garnish:
1½ dl / 5 oz lingonberry /
cranberry jam
1 Tbsp water
extra lingonberries/cranberries

A creamy cheesecake with a yuletide flavour. The ginger-thin base and tart Swedish lingonberries marry well with the vanilla-scented filling. It's best to bake this a day before serving. Serve cold.

Heat the oven to 150C/300F. Melt the butter. In a food processor, mix the ginger thins (or crush them to crumbs using a plastic bag and a fist!) and blend with the butter. Press the mixture onto the bottom and sides of a midsize springform pan. Cut the vanilla pod in half lengthwise and scrape out the seeds. Put them in a mixer bowl with the other filling ingredients and mix until smooth. Pour into the pie shell. Bake in the middle of the oven for 30–40 minutes until the pie has set. Let cool completely.

In a saucepan, melt the jam with a little water. Spread on the pie filling. Put in the fridge to set.

⊙ Have all ingredients at room temperature when you begin. Don't beat the eggs too much. Don't overbake. Follow these simple rules and your cheesecake will be creamy and without those unappealing cracks.

INDEX

INDEX BY CATEGORY

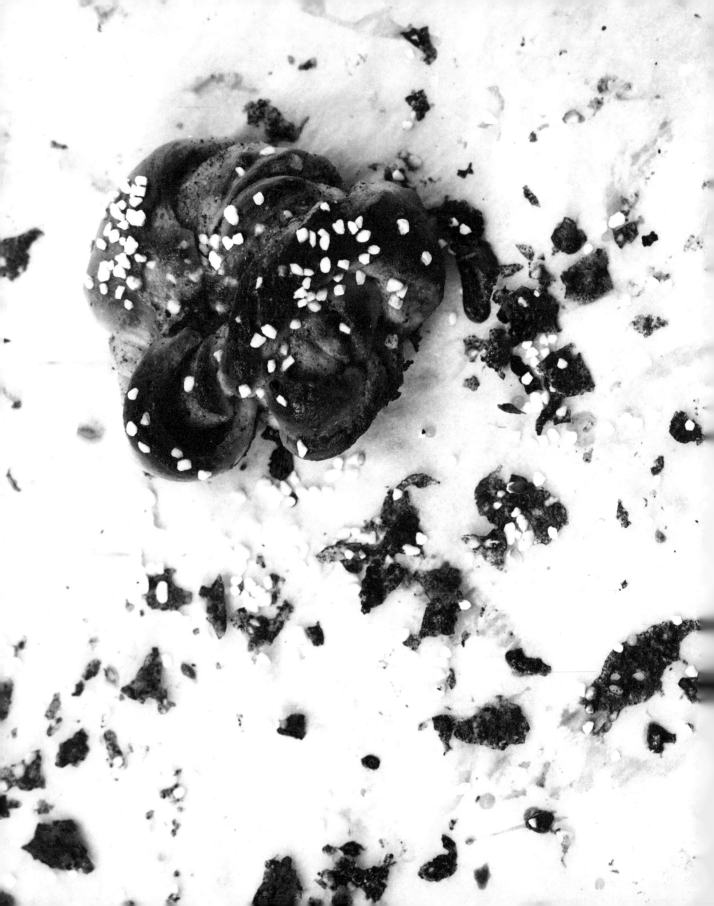